How to PAINT

house beautiful™
HOW TO PAINT

a complete guide to painting your home

COWLES
Creative Publishing, Inc.
Minnetonka, Minnesota, USA

HOW TO PAINT

Created by: The Editors of Cowles Creative Publishing, Inc., in cooperation with House Beautiful magazine.

House Beautiful™ is a trademark of Hearst Communications, Inc. Marketed by Wal-Mart Stores, Inc., Bentonville, AR 72716

President: Iain Macfarlane
Vice President, Custom Services: Sue Riley
Vice President, Photography & Production: Jim Bindas
Group Director, Book Development: Zoe Graul
Director, Custom Marketing and Publishing: Hugh Kennedy
Creative Director: Lisa Rosenthal
Senior Managing Editor: Elaine Perry
Senior Editor: Linda Neubauer
Writers: Sally Clark, Barbara Knox
Copy Editor: Janice Cauley
Senior Art Director: Stephanie Michaud
Contributing Art Director: Dawn Drilling
Prop Stylist: Christine Jahns
Photo Stylists: Jennifer Bailey, Bobbette Destiche
Studio Services Manager: Marcia Chambers
Photo Services Coordinator: Carol Osterhus
Photographers: Dennis Becker, John Lauenstein, Mark Macemon
Set Builders: Troy Johnston, Greg Wallace
Production Manager: Stasia Dorn

Editor in Chief: Louis Oliver Gropp
Editor: Margaret Kennedy
Managing Editor: Deborah L. Martin

For more information on House Beautiful magazine, visit their website at: *www.housebeautiful.com*

Hearst Magazines Brand Development
Senior Vice President: David Graff
Director of Licensing: Risa Turken
Licensing Manager: Karen Williams
Associate Licensing Manager: Jenifer Kramer

Photography Credits: Antoine Bootz (pp. 3-upper right, 4, 8-9, 20, 22, 42, 52, 54, 69-upper right), Langdon Clay (pp. 10-lower left, 68-upper left, 82-83), Michael Dunne (p. 10-upper right), David Frazier (p. 58), Kari Haavisto (pp. 66-67, back cover-upper right), Lizzie Himmel (pp. 3-lower right, 16-17, 19-lower right, back cover-lower right), Christopher Irion (p. 6-7), Jon Jensen (pp. 11-lower left, 62, cover), Peter Margonelli (p. 90-91), Tom McCavera (p. 64), Jeff McNamara (p. 56), David Phelps (p. 19-lower left), Lilo Raymond (p. 85), Walter Smalling (p. 19-upper right), John Vaughan (p. 19-upper left), Dominique Vorillon (pp. 8, 21, 48-49, 84, back cover-upper left, lower left), Judith Watts (pp. 12-13, 60)

Library of Congress Cataloging-in-Publication Data
How to paint: a complete guide to painting your home.
    p. cm.
    Includes index.
    ISBN 0-86573-190-X (softcover)
    1. House painting. I. Cowles Publishing Company.
TT320.H86 1998
698'.1--dc21   98-19866

Printed on American paper by:
  R. R. Donnelley & Sons Co.
01 00 99 98 / 5 4 3 2 1

Whenever I change the paint color of a room I momentarily panic, wondering if I've chosen well. Not until all the walls are finished and I live with it for about a week can I forget the former color and rejoice in the new.

Paint is decorating's most versatile element. A fresh coat of paint is the quickest way to make a tired room look young, a dark room seem brighter, and a cramped room seem more open. Paint can rescue an old floor by placing a carpet of sparkling color underfoot, and it can bring permanent sunshine to a space that may get little natural daylight.

Paint is magic in a can. It can wrap a room in a whisper of color or turn up the volume with a vibrant hue, creating a totally different look. Brush a ceiling with cool white and the space turns luminous; pick out the trim in contrasting colors and the room goes lively. Considering its reasonable cost, paint yields enormously rich results.

As the editor of House Beautiful, I've seen wonderful transformations achieved with paint. Today's vast range of colors encompasses every conceivable shade, from the most subtle tints to full-bodied rich hues. White alone is available in dozens of shades, from creamy tones with a hint of warm yellow to whites cooled with a tint of blue. The wealth of color choices makes decorating your home an exciting adventure.

This book is intended to help you achieve a thorough and professional look with any paint project you may be contemplating. It provides a step-by-step guide to choosing the correct type of paint, selecting the appropriate brushes and other equipment you may need, and preparing the area before you begin. Tricks of the trade, such as professional strategies for painting woodwork and doors, help make the project go more smoothly. Whether you are painting an interior or exterior, one room or a houseful of rooms, this guide will assist you in achieving an expert finish. And don't forget to follow your own color instincts so you'll end up living with rooms you love.

Margaret Kennedy

all about
PAINT

Today, paint is available in a wide variety of types and finishes. And your color choices are limited only by your imagination. Whether you want a tough, childproof finish or a soft, sophisticated wash of color, you'll find just the right paint on the shelf of your paint store.

These simple guidelines for choosing paint will help steer you toward the paint products necessary for the look you want.

The Southwest look in this dining room began with painting the walls a soft terra-cotta color.

TYPES OF PAINT

Paint falls into two basic categories:
water-base or oil-base paint. Both water-
base and oil-base paints are available in
various sheens, each recommended for
different areas of your house.

Virtually all interior painting jobs today
– including walls, ceilings, and woodwork
– are done using water-base paint, which
is commonly called latex paint. Water-
base paint is safer for the environment and easier to use than oil-
base paint. You can clean up brushes and rollers quickly with soap
and water, and just as easily remove spatters from your skin.
Latex paint dries quickly on the surface, so you can apply second
coats in a few hours. Most latex paints have comparatively mild
odors, so room ventilation is less of a concern.

Oil-base paints, also called alkyd paints, give a durable, smooth
finish. They do, however, require longer drying times, and,
because you must use harsh solvents like mineral spirits or
turpentine, cleanup is more complicated.

*Painting walls a full-bodied pastel such as pineapple, left, or periwinkle,
right, wraps a room in soft color.*

PAINT	CHARACTERISTICS AND APPLICATIONS
Flat latex	No sheen; for walls and ceilings
Satin latex	Low sheen; for walls, ceilings, trim
Semi-gloss latex	Slightly glossy sheen; for walls and trim; durable
High-gloss latex	Reflective sheen; for doors, cabinets, trim; washable, durable
Satin-enamel latex	Low sheen; smooth, hard finish; for trim and furniture
Gloss-enamel latex	Very glossy; smooth, hard finish; for trim and furniture
Oil-base enamels	Very glossy sheen; smooth, hard finish; for trim and furniture

PAINTING ROOM BY ROOM

Different areas of the house will benefit from different types of paint. Manufacturers generally label paint clearly if it is designed for a specific area, so always check labels carefully to confirm that you're buying the right paint.

Kitchen and Bath Paint

Because mildew and water damage are more likely in humid areas like these, specialized kitchen and bath paints are now available. These water-base paints typically come in a semi-gloss enamel finish that cleans easily and is moisture and peel resistant. The paints also contain additives to inhibit mildew growth.

Walls of pale ochre brighten a north-facing kitchen.

Children's Room Paint

Paint manufacturers have recently introduced nontoxic (always check the label) water-base paints designed for use in children's rooms, rec rooms, and other rooms children might use. Generally featuring a low-gloss enamel finish, these paints are resistant to household stains, fingerprints, and smudges. The finish is formulated to stand up to repeated cleanings with soap and water.

White-painted walls are a foil for lively striped accents.

Ceiling Paint

Thicker than standard water-base paints, ceiling paints are formulated to be spatter-resistant and nonyellowing. These paints, which also offer quick drying times, generally come in either a flat finish or a specialty, textured finish. The textured paints provide a nubby "popcorn-style" finish, which masks surface imperfections. Ceiling paints are available in white or bright white to give your ceiling maximum light reflectance. This is important, since ceilings tend to "read" darker than walls.

The dramatic height of a soaring space is underscored by using the same cream-toned paint on walls and ceiling.

Floor Paint

Water-base or oil-base floor paints are designed to withstand heavy traffic. Floor paints typically come in a scuff-resistant satin-enamel finish. Antislip additives can be mixed directly into the floor paint to provide a more slip-resistant surface.

White-painted floor adds an airy look to a summer house.

PRIMERS AND SEALERS

Unseen beneath the top paint coat, primers and sealers are nonetheless key ingredients in a quality paint job. Although they usually have very little pigment, these products help cover flaws and ensure that the paint adheres well to the surface. It is usually not necessary to prime a nonporous surface in good condition, like painted wood, painted plaster, or painted drywall.

Primers are available in both water-base and oil-base varieties. Different types are recommended for different jobs.

Flat Latex Primer
Used for sealing unfinished drywall or previously painted surfaces, this primer dries quickly so your top coat can be applied on the same day.

Deep Color Primer
When you plan to apply a very deep, dark color to your walls, prime first with this type of latex primer. It is designed to be tinted with a color similar to your top coat, and will provide better top coat coverage and appearance.

Latex Enamel Primer
Used primarily for sealing raw wood, enamel undercoat closes the pores of the wood and provides for a smooth top finish. Do not use the primer on cedar, redwood, or plywood that contains water-soluble dyes, because the dyes will bleed through the primer.

tip *Stain-killing sealers are available in spray cans for quick-and-easy spot priming.*

Stenciled stair risers are a subtle decoration in an all-white room.

Stain-killing Primer

Available in both alkyd and latex forms, these primers are designed to seal stains like crayon, ink, and grease so they will not bleed through your top coat of paint. Use them to seal knotholes in wood, and for cedar, redwood, and plywood that contain water-soluble dyes.

Metal and Masonry Primer

Designed specifically for use with metal, brick, or cement block surfaces, these latex primers can be used on the interior or exterior of your home.

You may find metal primers for both clean, rust-free metal surfaces and for surfaces where rusting has already occurred. Both types inhibit rusting and allow the top coat to adhere evenly to the metal.

PLANNING YOUR PROJECT

Timing

It is a good idea to estimate how long your painting project will take to complete. While every painter works at a different pace, remember that most projects take more time than originally planned and that preparation and drying times will affect your schedule. As a rule, preparation time takes longer than most people anticipate. If you are planning to work on weekends, for instance, complete your wall preparation on one weekend; the next weekend, you will be ready to move furniture, drape and mask surfaces, and apply paint.

TYPICAL DRYING TIMES		
	WATER-BASE	OIL-BASE
PRIMERS	1- 4 hours	4 - 10 hours; do not recoat for 24 hours
PAINTS	1- 4 hours	6 - 10 hours; do not recoat for 24 hours
STAINS	1- 4 hours	6 - 10 hours; do not recoat for 24 hours

COVERAGE

To calculate how much paint you will need to finish your project, use this standard formula. Work in square feet (or square meters).

1 **Measure each wall to figure the area:**
   height × width = area
   Add the wall totals together for the sum total of wall area.

2 **Measure each window and door to figure the area:**
   height × width = area
   Add the window and door areas together for the sum total of window and door area.

3 **Now subtract the total window and door area from the total wall area:**
   wall area
   - window/door area
   = total area of the wall
   space you will need to paint

4 **Measure ceilings and floors to figure total area you need to paint:**
   length × width = area

Most interior paint products are designed to cover approximately 400 square feet per gallon (36 square meters per 3.56 liters). To figure how many gallons of wall paint you will need, simply divide your total wall area by 400. (Check the paint can label for the manufacturer's coverage recommendation.) Don't forget to double your final amount if you plan to apply two coats.

all about
COLOR

Of all the decisions you make for your painting project, the one that will have the greatest impact is the color you choose. Because paint can be mixed in virtually any color you can find or imagine, choosing colors is also where the fun begins. With an understanding of color and the many approaches you can take, you'll be able to work color magic that expresses your personal decorating taste.

COLOR CHOICES

Begin narrowing your options by recognizing your personal color preferences. Current color trends are great, but only if they are a reflection of your taste. Take color inspiration from a host of sources, including movie sets, designer show houses, department store model rooms, or even a favorite scarf or piece of china. The colors that draw your attention may be the ones you want on your walls.

Unless you are starting with an empty house, your color options are greatly influenced by your existing furniture, window treatments, flooring, and even artwork. Your goal is to select paint colors that will bring the walls into harmony with all the room's elements and create a smooth color transition from room to room throughout the entire house.

Whether you prefer tried-and-true traditional schemes, trendy hues, or a dramatic palette of bold colors, you should consider some basic color rules.

◆ Cool colors (blues and greens) tend to be calming; warm colors (reds, yellows, and oranges) tend to be cheerful and uplifting. Consider both the mood you want as well as your climate when choosing warm or cool colors.

◆ Any color will look more intense when seen next to white.

◆ Complementary colors appear more intense when used side by side.

◆ Using light and dark colors side by side will intensify the effect of both.

Color Approaches

There are several standard color approaches to decorating. Each approach has its own style and its own effect on your mood.

Natural colors. Colors that mimic the hues seen in nature create restful, somewhat neutral, backgrounds for interiors. Since natural colors never go out of style, they are a very solid decorating choice. (top, left)

Contrasting colors. Pairing light colors with dark colors creates dramatic spaces. The classic combination is black and white, but any combination of dark and light will infuse a room with drama. Bringing contrasting colors into your rooms can be done easily by painting walls light and trim dark (or vice versa). (bottom, left)

Whites. White is never just white. Available in shades of cool blue-white to warm, creamy white, this classic room color can be used to create everything from soft, romantic spaces to crisp, contemporary backdrops. (top, right)

Bright colors. Bold, saturated colors enliven rooms. As a rule, reds seem exciting and dramatic; yellows are cheerful; and greens, restful. Bright colors can be used effectively to highlight architectural details; they are also fun when used in children's bedrooms or playrooms. (bottom, right)

Charcoal-painted crown moldings "frame" paler gray walls (top, left); against white walls, slate-blue moldings and door are country-style accents (bottom, left); continuing the white of the ceiling to overhead moldings creates an expansive feeling in a hallway (top, right); blue paint wakes up 1950s pine panelling (bottom, right).

The colors you paint your walls will affect your comfort level, your mood, and your perceptions of space. With a little preplanning, you can use these facts to your advantage.

For instance, a long, narrow room can be made to appear wider by painting the short walls a darker color than the long walls. Light colors expand space; dark colors advance into the room. Likewise, cool colors are room expanding; warm colors eat up space. Using this same phenomenon, you can raise the ceiling in a room simply by painting it a lighter color than the walls or by bringing the lighter ceiling color down onto the wall to picture-rail level.

It's a psychological fact that social gatherings are more energized in a room filled with warm colors. Appetites stir and conversation comes alive in a red dining room. In contrast, pale blues and greens are perfect for bedrooms because of their calming effect. If you are planning on painting the nursery, consider whether your intention is to stimulate your child or create a quiet, restful place for sleeping. Perhaps bright primary colors are better choices for the playroom.

You don't have to paint every room in your house the same color, even if you've followed that rule with the flooring. You can develop a natural transition from room to room, by selecting related colors, however. The pale, sunny colors used in the kitchen may change to deeper golds in the dining room. You may walk from a teal-blue family room onto a sky-blue porch. A neutral-colored hallway can be the perfect transition into bedrooms of various colors.

Choosing an adventurous paint color gives a room a youthful spirit—even in an older house.

HOW TO SELECT PAINT COLORS

Before you settle on your color choices, consider these key elements:

◆ **Furnishings.** Will the walls be a backdrop for show-stopping furniture pieces, like fine antiques or contemporary classics, or do you need wall color to bring interest to plain furnishings?

◆ **Ceilings.** White ceilings give the room a sense of height. For a little coziness, you might apply a lighter shade of the wall color to the ceiling. Remember that the ceiling tends to "read" darker than the walls.

◆ **Room details.** Painting woodwork and other architectural details a contrasting color will highlight interesting moldings and decorative details. On the other hand, you may not want to bring attention to damaged or plain woodwork by using a strong accent color.

Buying Your Paint

The paint colors you see in the store will look different in your home. Lighting conditions and room furnishings will affect the way the color will appear. Before you buy large quantities of paint, do some simple tests.

1 Bring paint chips home and put them on the surfaces where they will be used, so you can see how light affects them.

2 Create your own professional-style "color board" by cutting your paint samples into the right proportions (largest for walls, then progressively smaller for ceilings, floors, and trim). Tape them together onto a piece of cardboard, and view them in the room you plan to paint.

3 Buy a small quantity of paint in the color you want. Test your color choice by painting a large sheet of tagboard and taping it to the wall. Study it in daylight and evening light. Mount a wall test patch and a smaller trim test patch

side by side to see how one affects the other.

4 If you plan to use different colors for the base coat and the top coat of your walls or trim, test this combination before making your final color selection.

5 When you can't find just the right color in the manufacturer's paint chips, request a custom color. Most paint stores can blend custom colors based on such samples as fabric swatches or ceramic tiles. There may be a small fee for blending custom colors. Be sure to buy a small amount of the custom-colored paint and test it at home before investing in large quantities.

the right
TOOLS

For most home improvement projects, choosing the right tools for the job is half the battle. Painting is no different. So before you grab the first brush or roller cover you spot on the store shelf, bone up on some basics. Because of the abundance of quality, specialized painting products on the market today, you'll have no trouble finding the right tools for your job. With this information, you'll know how to make the best choices.

ROLLERS

A good roller can be invaluable to your painting project. Inexpensive and efficient, this simple tool can save you time and energy. Rollers are commonly used for painting large wall areas, ceilings, and floors. Two simple components make up the roller: the frame and the cover. Covers are easily changeable, according to the job at hand.

Selecting a Roller Frame

Choose a standard 9-inch (23 cm) roller with wire frame and nylon bearings to be certain it rolls smoothly. Check the handle to make sure the molded grip is comfortable in your hand. The handle should also have a threaded end so you can attach an extension handle for painting ceilings and high walls.

Selecting a Roller Cover

Roller covers, or pads, come in either synthetic or natural lamb's wool, and are available in a variety of nap thicknesses. In general, synthetic covers are used for water-base paint; lamb's-wool covers are used for oil-base paint. Select roller covers with longer-lasting plastic, rather than cardboard, cores.

Short-nap roller covers have ¼-inch to ⅜-inch (6 mm to 1 cm) nap. Choose short-nap covers for applying glossy paints to smooth surfaces like wallboard, wood, and smooth plaster.

Medium-nap roller covers have ½-inch to ¾-inch (1.3 to 2 cm) nap. These are commonly called all-purpose covers. They give flat surfaces a slight texture and are a good choice for walls and ceilings with small imperfections.

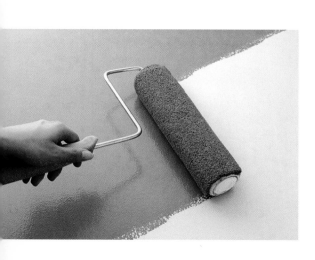

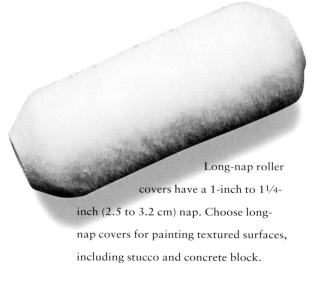

Long-nap roller covers have a 1-inch to 1¼-inch (2.5 to 3.2 cm) nap. Choose long-nap covers for painting textured surfaces, including stucco and concrete block.

Specialty Rollers

Roller covers are available in sizes up to 18 inches (46 cm) for painting large open surfaces quickly. However, these longer covers are heavier and more difficult to handle. There are also rollers and pads available for painting edges, corners, and other specific jobs.

Roller Accessories

Extension handles are needed for painting ceilings and high walls. Various types are available, including wood or adjustable, lightweight metal handles.

Roller trays with legs are designed to sit steadily on the shelf of a stepladder. A good tray will resist flexing when it's twisted. A textured ramp will keep the roller moving easily.

For large jobs, you may want a 5-gallon bucket with a roller screen. Load the roller by dipping it straight into the paint, then rolling it along the screen to remove excess.

A 1½ -inch (3.8 cm) trim brush works well for painting narrow woodwork.

A 2-inch (5 cm) trim brush works well for painting woodwork and windows.

Choose a 2-inch (5 cm) tapered sash brush for painting windows.

Choose a 4-inch (10 cm) brush for painting walls and ceilings.

BRUSHES

Paintbrushes fall into two basic categories: natural bristle and synthetic bristle. Do not assume that natural is better, which was once the common wisdom about paintbrushes. In fact, natural-bristle brushes should only be used with alkyd, or oil-base, paint. If natural-bristle brushes are used with water-base paints, the bristles will bunch together. Choose synthetic-bristle brushes for water-base latex paints.

Look for quality. A bargain brush will save you a few dollars up front, but may well cost you more in the long run. Invest in a few quality brushes; with proper care, they should last through many paint projects. As a starting point, choose a straight-edged 3-inch (7.5 cm) wall brush, a 2-inch (5 cm) straight-edged trim brush, and a tapered sash brush.

A good brush has a strong, hardwood handle. Dense bristles should be flagged, or split, at the ends. Always check to make sure the bristles are

attached securely to the handle. If some pull out when you tug, you can expect the bristles to fall out into your paint job. The metal band, or ferrule, should be firmly attached. Inside the bristles, check that the spacer plugs are made of wood, not cardboard, which may soften when wet.

PAINT PADS

Paint pads come in a wide variety of shapes and sizes to accommodate many different tasks. Use these foam pads with water-base paints. Small pads with tapered edges are helpful for painting narrow areas like window trim or louvers, while the larger sizes can be used on wall surfaces. Specialty pads are available for painting corners and hard-to-reach areas. Paint pads generally apply paint in a thinner coat than a brush or roller, so additional coats may be necessary.

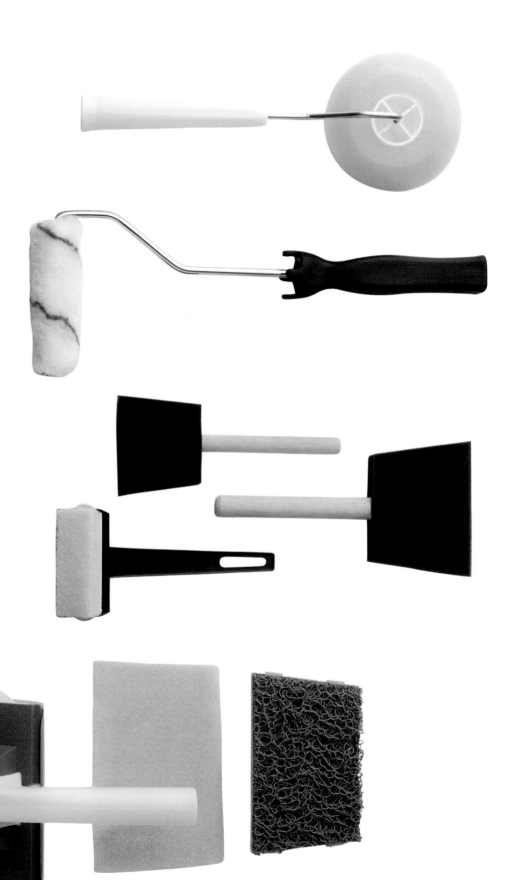

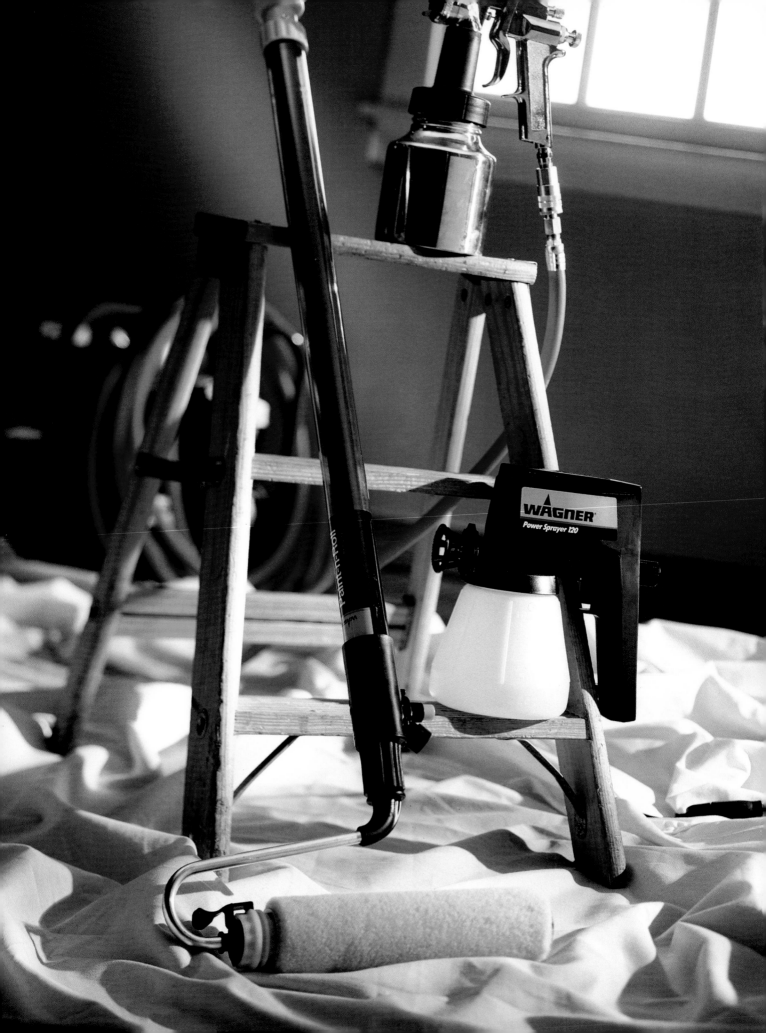

SPECIALTY TOOLS

Paint Sprayers

There are two basic types of paint sprayer. Airless paint sprayers, most commonly seen at home improvement stores, have an electric pump that creates the paint spray. Air paint sprayers use compressed air to generate the paint spray. All sprayers produce some over-spray, so wear protective gear and mask off surrounding areas that could be spattered. Anything movable, like cabinet doors, should be painted outside or in a workroom, when possible. Thinning your paint slightly will make the sprayer easier to use and provide more even coverage. Be sure to clean the sprayer very thoroughly to avoid clogging the works permanently.

Power Rollers

Designed to pump paint directly onto the roller cover from the paint can, power rollers can speed a large paint job along. Most power roller kits, available at home improvement centers, include either a reservoir or special paint can cover, a pump, a hose, an extension handle, and roller covers. Remember that both set-up and cleanup will be more time-consuming than using a standard roller.

Painter's mitts are very useful for painting things like pipes, radiators, and other contoured surfaces that are awkward to paint with a brush.

Wear safety goggles to protect your eyes while repairing surfaces, using chemical cleaning products, or painting overhead.

Use an approved mask to filter vapors if your work area is not adequately ventilated. Check the product label for toxicity warnings.

LADDERS AND SCAFFOLDING

Build a basic interior scaffold by running an extension plank through the steps of two stepladders. Buy a 2 × 10 plank no more than 12 feet (3.7 m) long, or rent a plank from a hardware or rental equipment store. The ladders should face away from one another so that the steps are to the inside. To use a scaffold on a stairway, run the extension plank through the step of a ladder, and place the other end on a stair step. Check the plank to be sure it is level. Whenever possible, keep the plank close to the wall.

Ladder Safety

✦ Never stand on the top step, top brace, or the utility shelf of a stepladder.

✦ Make sure your ladder is steady and on level ground; double-check that the ladder braces are completely down and locked into place.

✦ Keep your weight centered on the ladder, which should be in front of you as you work, so that you can lean into it for balance.

✦ Check the ladder steps periodically; tighten the bolts on the braces as necessary.

✦ Move your ladder frequently as you work so you aren't tempted to overreach, which could cause the ladder to tip.

preparing the
SURFACE

Preparation is the key to a good paint job. Taking the time to repair, clean, and prime your walls, floors, and ceilings will guarantee a longer-lasting paint finish. Because dirt and grease will interfere with a good, smooth paint finish, every surface should be thoroughly cleaned before painting.

Remember, don't rush the preparation process and you'll be rewarded with a beautiful, durable finish once the project is completed.

CLEAN THE SURFACE FIRST

To avoid messy streaking, begin washing your walls from the bottom up. While you can use common household cleansers for the job, many professional painters use a TSP (trisodium phosphate) solution.

Wearing rubber gloves, wash with a damp, not dripping, sponge. Rinse thoroughly with clean water. After the surface is dry, sand lightly where needed, then wipe the surface with a clean cloth.

As you clean, you will discover any small problems, like cracks or stains, on the surface. Make those repairs before beginning to paint.

SURFACE PREPARATION AT A GLANCE		
SURFACE TO BE PAINTED	PREPARATION	PRIMER
UNFINISHED WOOD	1. Sand surface smooth 2. Wipe with tack cloth to remove grit 3. Apply primer	Latex enamel undercoat
PAINTED WOOD	1. Clean surface to remove grease and dirt 2. Rinse with clear water; let dry 3. Sand surface lightly to degloss, smooth, and remove loose paint 4. Wipe with tack cloth to remove grit 5. Apply primer to bare wood spots	Latex enamel undercoat only on areas of bare wood
UNFINISHED WALLBOARD	1. Dust with hand broom, or vacuum with soft brush 2. Apply primer	Flat latex primer
PAINTED WALLBOARD	1. Clean surface to remove dirt and grease 2. Rinse with clear water; allow to dry 3. Apply primer only if making a dramatic color change	Not necessary, except when painting over spot repairs, or dark or strong color; then use flat latex primer
UNPAINTED PLASTER	1. Sand surfaces as necessary 2. Dust with hand broom, or vacuum with soft brush	Polyvinyl acrylic primer
PAINTED PLASTER	1. Clean surface to remove dirt and grease 2. Rinse with clear water; allow to dry 3. Repair any cracks or holes 4. Sand surface to smooth and degloss	Not necessary, except on spot repairs or when painting over strong or dark colors; then use polyvinyl acrylic primer

Preparing the Surface

Water Stains

PROBLEM: Unsightly water or rust stains require immediate attention because they may indicate a leak somewhere.

SOLUTION: Check for leaking pipes or damaged flashing on the roof. Before you paint, repair the leak. If the wall surface is soft or crumbling, repair the area (pages 40 to 43). To seal and cover a water-stained area that is not otherwise damaged, use a stain-sealing primer that contains shellac. If left unsealed, the stain will eventually show through your new paint job.

Colored Stains

PROBLEM: Black marks and other wall stains like crayon or marker are not always easily removed.

SOLUTION: Apply a stain remover to a clean, dry cloth and rub lightly on the stain. Cover any stain that is not completely removed with a stain-sealing primer that contains shellac.

tip **SAFETY:** *Always wear rubber gloves and eye protection when using cleaning products like bleach or ammonia.*

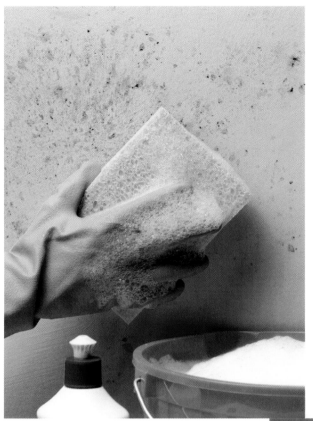

Mildew and Mold

PROBLEM: Because mold and mildew grow in damp areas, check kitchen and bathroom surfaces carefully.

SOLUTION: Test the stain by washing it with water and detergent. If it is mildew, it will not wash away. Wash the area with a solution of 1 part chlorine bleach to 4 parts water, which will kill the mildew spores. Scrub with a soft-bristle brush. Then wash the mildew away with a TSP solution, rinse with clear water, and allow the area to dry thoroughly before painting.

Peeling Paint

PROBLEM: Peeling paint occurs for a number of reasons, and it must be removed before you repaint.

SOLUTION: Scrape away the loose paint with a putty knife or paint scraper. Apply a thin coat of spackle to the edges of the chipped paint, using a putty knife. Sand the area with 150-grit sandpaper, creating a smooth transition between bare wall and surrounding painted surfaces. Wipe clean with a damp sponge. Spot-prime the area with PVA primer.

Always complete minor repairs before you begin priming and painting. These common drywall problems are easily solved with some basic tools and materials.

Filling Small Nail Holes

1   Using a putty knife or your finger, force a small amount of drywall compound or spackle into the hole, filling it completely. Scrape the area smooth with the putty knife and let dry.

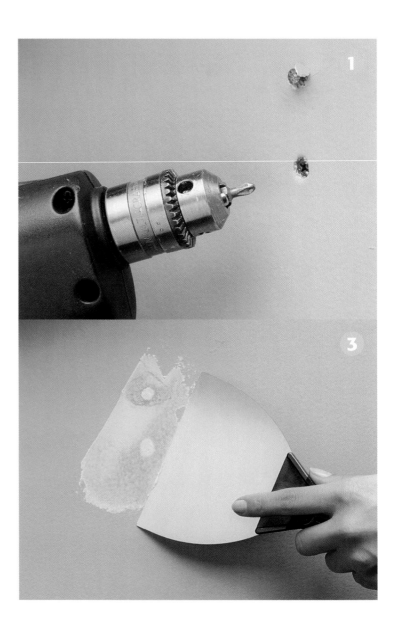

2   Sand the area lightly with 150-grit sandpaper. Wipe clean with a damp sponge, let dry, and dab on polyvinyl acrylic (PVA) primer.

Fixing Popped Drywall Nails

Drywall nails can work themselves loose, either popping through the drywall or creating a small bulge on the surface.

1   Drive a new wallboard screw into place 2" (5 cm) below the popped nail, sinking the head slightly below the wall surface. Be sure the screw hits the stud and pulls the drywall tight against the framing, taking care not to damage the drywall surface.

2   Scrape away loose paint or drywall material around the popped nail. Drive the popped nail back into the framing, sinking the head slightly below the drywall surface.

3   Using a drywall knife, cover both the nail hole and the new screw hole with spackle. Sand and prime the patched areas.

Filling Dents and Gouges in Drywall ▶

1 Scrape away any drywall paper, using a drywall knife, if necessary. Sand the dented or gouged area lightly. Using a drywall knife, fill the dent or hole with spackle. For deep holes or dents, build up the spackle in layers, allowing each layer to dry before adding another.

2 Sand the patched area with fine-grit sandpaper; seal the area with PVA primer.

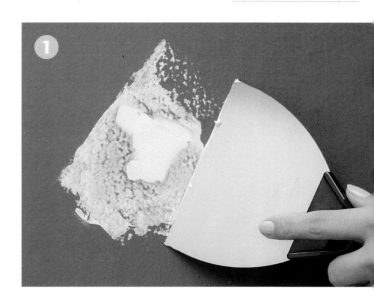

Patching Holes in Drywall ▼

1 For a larger problem, cut a neat rectangle around the hole, using a drywall saw. Cut backer strips from drywall or wood; insert them into the opening and secure them to the back of the opening, using hot glue.

2 Cut a rectangular drywall patch slightly smaller than the opening; secure it in place to the backing strips, using hot glue.

3 Apply self-adhesive drywall tape over the cracks; then apply spackle. After drying, sand the area smooth and apply PVA primer.

4 Self-adhering fiberglass and metal repair patches (below) are available for quick-and-easy repairs. Simply apply the patch over the hole. Then coat the area with spackle, blending into the surrounding wall. After drying, sand it smooth and apply primer.

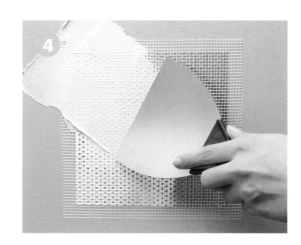

TROUBLESHOOTING PLASTER WALLS

Since drywall was not introduced into new home building until after World War II, many homes have plaster walls, which tend to crack and chip over time. These common problems can be fixed with basic tools and materials.

For a subtle sheen, satin-finish beige paint was applied to this bedroom's plaster walls; to add definition, ceiling molding was painted in contrasting white paint with a semi-gloss finish.

Repairing Cracks in Plaster

1 Scrape away any loose plaster or textured surface along the crack. Reinforce the crack by applying self-adhesive fiberglass drywall tape.

2 Apply a thin layer of joint compound over the taped crack, using a taping knife or trowel. Allow it to dry. Apply a second thin coat, if necessary to hide the tape edges.

3 Sand the area lightly, using 150-grit sandpaper. Apply PVA primer. Retexture the surface, using texturized paint (page 64), if necessary.

Repairing Holes in Plaster

1 Gently scrape away any loose material and clean the damaged area. Undercut the edges of the hole where possible.

2 Cut a small piece of wire lath to fit the damaged area and staple it to the existing wood lath. Mix a small amount of patching plaster, following the manufacturer's directions.

3 Using a drywall knife or trowel, apply the plaster to the wire lath in a thin coat, working the material under the edges of the hole.

4 Score a grid pattern into the surface of the patching plaster with the tip of your knife; allow to dry.

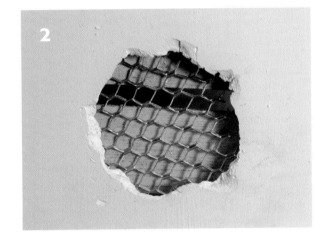

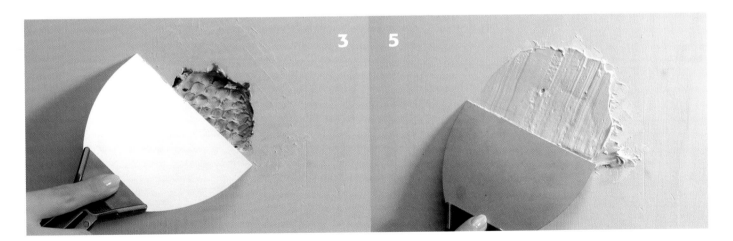

5 To apply a second coat, first dampen the area with a sponge, then apply another layer of patching plaster, even with the surrounding wall. Allow it to dry thoroughly.

6 Sand the area lightly, using 150-grit sandpaper. Apply PVA primer. Retexture the surface, using texturized paint (page 64).

TROUBLESHOOTING PROBLEMS IN WOODWORK

Stripping Wood

If the old paint on your woodwork is heavily layered or badly chipped, strip it before repainting.

Chemical Strippers

Wear protective gear, including eye protection, gloves, and a respirator mask. Every chemical stripper will have its own recommendations for use: follow the label directions and work in a well-ventilated area.

Power Sanders

Use a coarse-grit paper to strip the wood with a power sander, and sand in the direction of the grain. Change paper frequently as paint will gum up on the surface of your sander. Finish by hand-sanding with a fine-grit paper.

Heat Guns

Hold the gun near the wood to soften the paint just until it begins to blister, then remove paint with a scraper. Keep heat in front of your scraper as you work. Do not overheat the surface, which could scorch the wood.

Repairing Painted Wood

1 Wash woodwork with a TSP solution, rinse, and let dry. Scrape away loose paint and sand edges to blend with surrounding areas.

2 Use a putty knife to apply glazing compound or wood putty to any nail holes, cracks, or dents; allow to dry.

3 Sand with 180-grit sandpaper. Wipe clean with a tack cloth, and prime.

Repairing Varnished Wood

1 Wearing rubber gloves, clean surfaces with mineral spirits and a soft rag.

2 Using a putty knife, fill nail holes or cracks with wood filler or glazing compound tinted to match the existing finish.

3 Sand patched areas smooth with 150-grit paper and wipe clean with a tack cloth.

4 Restain the patched areas to match the surrounding wood. Finish by applying one or two coats of varnish.

tip **SAFETY:** *Never use a heat gun to strip wood after you have applied a chemical stripper; the chemical residue may be vaporized or ignited by the heat.*

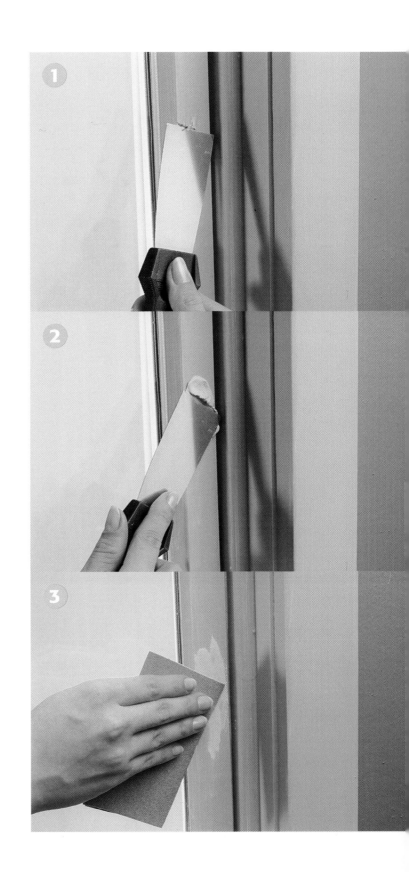

PREPARING THE ROOM

Once your repairs have been made, you're almost ready to paint. Take the time now to remove or cover anything in the room that could be spattered by paint as you work. Furniture should be moved into the center of the room and draped with plastic (readily available in large sheets at hardware stores and home improvement centers). Cover floors with canvas drop cloths (paint will not pool up on canvas like it will on plastic), and remove things like switch plates, window and door hardware, duct covers, and wall lights. Use tape to mask off wood moldings. Taking the time to mask and drape thoroughly will save both cleanup time and unnecessary damage to furnishings and fixtures.

tip **EFFICIENCY:**
Tape screws to their appropriate fixtures or hardware, so you can locate them quickly when you're ready to replace them.

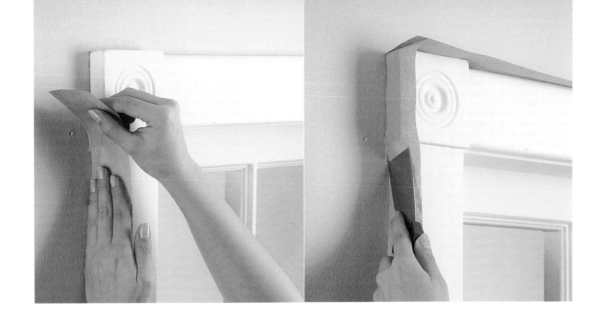

Taping

It is always wise to protect areas like woodwork and window glass that butt up against the surfaces you'll be painting. While taping these areas is not essential, it may save you cleanup time and will ensure a clean, straight finish. To mask woodwork, use painter's tape, which is a wide strip of brown paper with adhesive along one edge. Cut off short lengths of the tape, and, working one section at a time, smooth the adhesive edge onto the woodwork with a putty knife. Keep your edges as straight as possible. The paper edge will stick out past the molding, protecting it from paint spatters.

Painter's masking tape (not to be confused with the masking tape used for packages) is specially designed to be applied and removed without damaging painted surfaces. Still, it's best not to leave the tape in place longer than necessary. Wait until your paint is dry before removing the tape, otherwise the wet paint may leak over onto the adjacent areas. Look for these masking tapes in the paint section of your home improvement store. They are available in a wide range of widths and are often colored red or blue.

Draping

When painting the ceiling only, drape your walls with sheet plastic to prevent damage from paint spatters. Use 2-inch (5 cm) masking tape to hold the plastic sheets to the wall along the ceiling line.

Cover light fixtures

To protect hanging fixtures, unscrew the collar from the ceiling and lower it to expose the rough opening in the ceiling. Then wrap the fixture with a plastic bag.

paint paint
PAINT!

A new coat of paint can transform a room from dreary to dramatic. We'll teach you the secrets the professionals use, so that your paint projects can be outstanding.

From opening the can to laying on the last brush stroke of color, there are countless tricks of the trade to make the work go smoothly. With your surfaces repaired and primed, you're ready to go!

Lavender-blue window frames and shutters give a room an open-to-nature freshness.

TIME TO PRIME

Primers are used to seal surfaces that
will be painted. Patched areas and drywall
seams may absorb paint at different rates than
the surrounding areas; consequently, these spots will
show through a painted finish if not primed first.
Likewise, unfinished drywall should always be
primed first to ensure good coverage with
your top coat.

Woodwork

Always seal raw woodwork by applying a latex enamel primer before
laying on your painted finish. If you are painting over previously
painted woodwork, roughen the glossy surface with fine sandpaper
first, then spot-prime where areas of raw wood show through. Seal
textured surfaces with a polyvinyl acrylic, or PVA, primer. Apply with
a long-nap roller cover.

Unfinished Drywall

In cases of new construction or remodeling, you will have unfinished drywall surfaces. Seal these surfaces with a flat latex primer tinted to match your finish coat. Your paint dealer should be able to custom-tint the primer for you. Apply the primer using a brush for cutting in edges and a medium-nap roller cover for wall surfaces.

Using Old Paint

If you plan to use previously opened paint, make sure it is free of lumps and debris. Cover a bucket with a section of cheesecloth or a nylon screen, and pour the paint through this filter. Any dirt or hardened paint bits will catch in the filter.

Thinning Paint

If you need to thin paint, pour a small amount of your paint into a bucket. Add thinner in very small amounts, mixing as you go, until you've achieved the right consistency.

Mixing The Paint

Always have your new paint shaken in the machine at the store; that will help you stir it at home later. Before opening the can, shake it again with your hands.

After you open the can, mix the paint thoroughly with a wooden stir stick. Or use a paint mixer bit, which attaches to a power drill, set on low speed. For large jobs, mix two cans of paint together in a large pail to avoid any slight color variations between cans. This is called boxing the paint. You can mix them in a smaller container by pouring small amounts of paint from each can into the bucket, stirring, and returning the paint to the cans. Repeat this procedure until both cans of paint have been completely mixed.

tip

SAFETY: *Paint cans usually carry the warning "use with adequate ventilation." This means that there should be no more vapor buildup inside than there would be if you were painting outside. Open doors and windows, or use an exhaust fan. If you can still smell bothersome solvents or paint, wear an approved ventilator mask (see page 31).*

The sun never sets in this living room whose colorful scheme began with vibrant yellow walls.

USING YOUR PAINTBRUSH

✦ Transfer some paint from the can into a small paint bucket with a handle. It will be easier to carry with you as you move around the room.

✦ Double-check your paintbrush. If you are using water-base (latex) paint, you should have a synthetic-bristle brush.

✦ Don't overload your paintbrush! Dip the bristles only about 2 inches (5 cm) into the paint. Tap, don't drag, the bristles on the side of the can.

1 Begin painting with horizontal strokes in a back-and-forth manner, using first one side of the brush, then the other. Press the brush against the surface just hard enough to flex the bristles slightly. Always paint from dry areas back into wet areas to avoid lap marks.

2 Smooth the paint evenly across the surface using vertical strokes. Feather, or blend, the edges of your painted area by brushing lightly with just the tip of your brush.

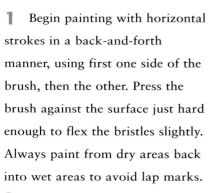

3 Along edges where a wall meets the ceiling or woodwork, use a technique called "cutting in." Hold the brush at a slight angle. Stroking slowly, move the brush slightly away from your edge as you go. This will allow paint to bead up along the straight line of the edge.

tip **TECHNIQUE:** *To avoid messy paint buildup in the groove of your paint can, pound several small nail holes into the groove. This will allow paint to drip back into the can.*

USING YOUR PAINT ROLLER

✦ Paint surfaces in small sections, working from dry surfaces back into wet paint to avoid roller marks.

✦ If you do notice roller marks, or lines of beaded paint, beginning to form on your paint job, feather the edges immediately before they dry. Try easing up on the pressure you're applying to the roller to avoid any further roller marks.

✦ If your paint job will take more than one day, cover the roller tightly with plastic wrap overnight to prevent the paint from drying out. Be sure to run the roller over a piece of scrap material before you begin painting again the next day.

A spirited paint color, like this offbeat khaki shade, tends to "fill up" walls, eliminating the need for artwork.

1 Load your roller by dipping it into the paint tray, then rolling it back and forth gently on the textured ramp to distribute the paint evenly. The roller cover should be soaked but not dripping when you start to paint.

2 With the loaded roller settled comfortably in your hand, roll paint onto the surface in smooth, crisscrossing strokes. When working on walls, roll upward on your first stroke to avoid spilling paint.

3 Distribute the paint across the surface using horizontal back-and-forth strokes.

4 Smooth the painted area by lightly drawing the roller down the surface, from top to bottom. Lift the roller at the bottom of each stroke, and then return to the top.

PAINTING CEILINGS AND WALLS

✦ When you are planning to paint an entire room, paint ceilings first, then woodwork, and walls last. Paint ceilings across the narrow width of the room first.

✦ Start painting ceilings near a window, and work back across the room. Keeping the natural light in front of you allows you to see your work as you go; you'll be more likely to notice mistakes.

✦ Avoid spattering problems by working at a slow, steady pace. Do not overload or fast-spin the roller.

A lilac-painted ceiling (left) gives a tall room a serene mood; contrasting white woodwork gives architectural definition to beams and windows.

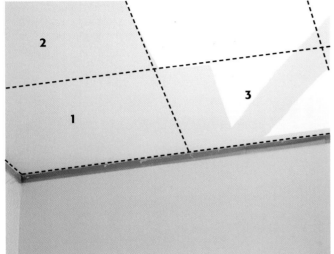

Painting Ceilings

1 Using a narrow brush, cut in a 3-inch (7.5 cm) strip of paint along one section of the ceiling's edge. Begin in the corner farthest from the entry door.

2 Using your roller with an extension handle, start painting in one corner. Paint in small sections about 3 × 3 feet (0.95 × 0.95 cm). Apply the paint with zigzag strokes, then distribute it evenly with back-and-forth strokes. Feather the edges by lifting the roller at the end of each sweep.

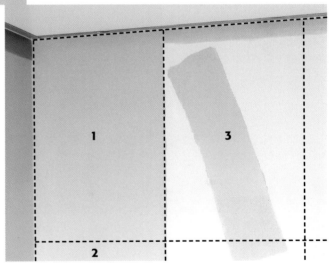

Painting Walls

1 Using a narrow brush, cut in a 2-inch (5 cm) strip of paint where the walls meet woodwork and ceiling. Begin in the upper right-hand corner if you are right-handed, upper left if you are left-handed. (This helps you avoid smearing paint if you accidentally lean into the wall as you work.)

2 Using your roller, paint one small wall section at a time. Work on the wall sections while your edges are still wet. When painting near the cut-in edge, slide the roller cover slightly off the roller. This helps to cover the cut-in edge as much as possible, since brushed paint dries to a different finish than rolled-on paint. Continue painting adjacent wall sections, cutting in with a brush and then rolling wall areas. Work from top to bottom. All finish strokes should be rolled toward the door.

 tip **SAFETY:** *Wearing a hat will help protect your head from inevitable paint spatters. Always wear eye protection when painting overhead.*

PAINTING DOORS

General Tips

✦ Remove doors whenever possible and lay them flat across two sawhorses to paint them.

✦ Remove hardware like doorknobs and lock sets; label the parts and keep them together in a plastic bag so you can locate them quickly when you are ready to replace them.

✦ Because mistakes are more apparent on doors than anywhere else, use a brush rather than a roller, and always apply paint in the direction of the grain.

✦ Choose door colors based on this rule: paint the door face to match the color of the room trim as seen when the door is closed. Do this even if the door is generally kept open. When the door's two faces are painted different colors (a common occurrence), paint the latch edge the same color as the trim of the room into which the door opens.

Painting cabinets and door deep contrasting colors enriches a country kitchen.

1 Paint the edges of the door first. Wipe off any paint that drips onto the door face, checking both sides of the door. On flat doors, work from top to bottom, and paint in the direction of the grain.

2 Troubleshoot problems as you go: because runs are especially common on doors, check the surface a few minutes after you've finished painting, and paint out any small runs before the paint has a chance to dry. Check the grooves in molding for any areas where paint has collected, and paint out excess. If you notice a run after the paint has already started to dry, let it dry completely, then sand the area smooth, and wipe clean with a tack cloth. Touch up the spot with more paint.

3 On panel doors, paint the beveled edges of the panels first (above, left); then paint the faces of the panels before the edges dry (above, right). Next paint horizontal rails (below, left), and finish by painting vertical styles (below, right). Always brush in the direction of the grain.

4 To apply a second coat, make sure paint is completely dry, sand lightly, and wipe clean with a tack cloth. Then lay on your second coat.

tip **SAFETY:** *If your home was built before 1978, you may have lead paint on your woodwork and walls. Purchase a lead-testing kit at your paint store. Have a qualified professional remove any lead paint.*

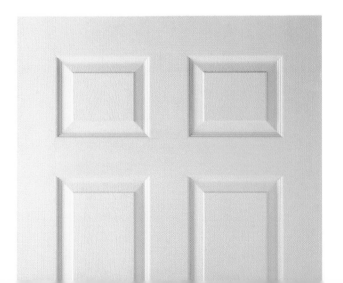

PAINTING WINDOWS AND MOLDINGS

General Tips

◆ Paint wood trim and windows before painting walls.

◆ Use 2-inch (5 cm) flat and 2-inch (5 cm) tapered sash brushes for painting woodwork and windows.

◆ Paint decorative carved moldings with a stiff-bristle stencil brush; use small, circular strokes to penetrate the recesses of the carving.

◆ Remove shelves wherever possible before painting built-in bookcases and cabinetry.

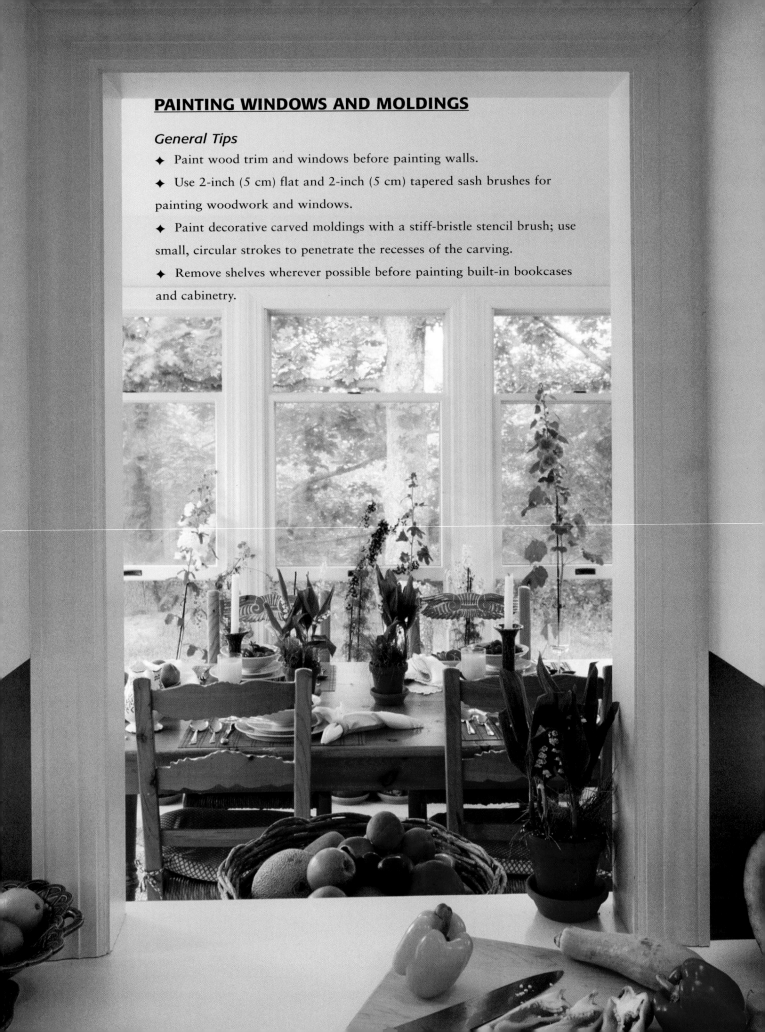

Painting a Window

1 Remove the window from the frame whenever possible. If you cannot remove the window, first take off all hardware, clean, and store in a labeled plastic bag. Using a 2-inch (5 cm) tapered sash brush, begin by painting the wood next to the glass. Use the narrow edge of the brush and overlap paint onto the glass to create a weather seal.

2 Clean excess paint off the window immediately with a putty knife wrapped in a clean cloth. Rewrap the knife often.

3 Paint the flat portions of the sashes, then the case moldings, sill, and apron; always work in the direction of the grain.

4 Move window up and down several times during the drying period to keep it from sticking. Use a putty knife to move the window to avoid touching painted surfaces.

5 Wait 24 hours to be sure the sashes have completely dried, then paint the upper half of the jam; allow to dry completely. Push the sashes up, and paint the lower jam; allow it to dry completely before closing the window.

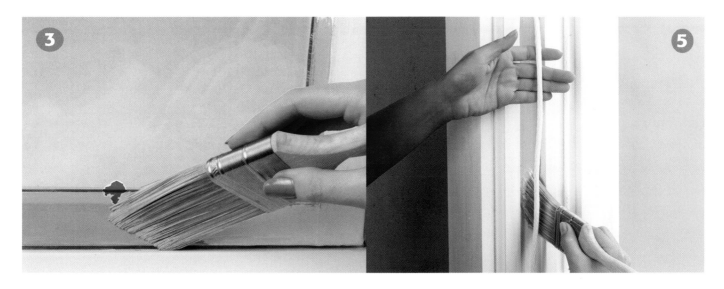

The white-painted trim of a window wall (left) provides an understated finish and does not intrude on the vista of nature seen from a breakfast room.

Against sage green walls, the summery effect of a white floor is underscored by painting shoe molding and windows white, too.

PAINTING FLOORS

General Tips

◆ Use only paints formulated for decks and floors; standard paints will not stand up to the constant wear and tear.

◆ Repair damaged floor areas before painting, and remove the shoe molding (the narrow strip of molding at the bottom of the baseboard) before painting.

◆ Clean floors thoroughly with a TSP solution and allow to dry; sand any small areas that have loose or peeling paint.

◆ Vacuum or dust windowsills and baseboards to make sure dirt and dust don't fall down into your paint job.

◆ Vacuum or sweep floor thoroughly just prior to painting.

tip SAFETY: *Using a thick piece of foam rubber, a gardening mat, or knee pads will avoid some wear and tear on your knees as you cut in edges along the baseboards.*

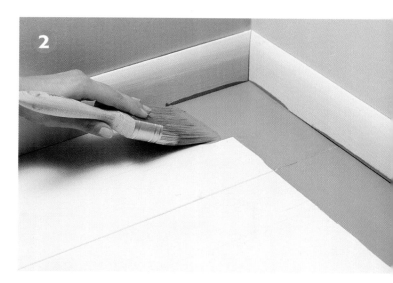

1 In areas where you are concerned about slippage, use an antislip additive with your floor paint. Made of pumice, these additives can be mixed directly into your paint (you will need to stir the paint frequently) or sprinkled onto the still-wet painted surface. Follow the manufacturer's directions for use on the can's label.

2 Using a 3-inch (7.5 cm) brush, cut in a painted edge along both sides of the corner farthest from the door.

3 Using a roller with an extension handle, apply paint in the section you have outlined. Work in the direction of the floor boards. To distribute paint evenly, roll across the floor boards you have just painted. Do not reload the roller.

4 Continue painting the floor one section at a time, remembering to feather edges and work from dry into wet areas to avoid lap marks.

5 Tack the shoe molding back into place when the floors are completely dry.

TEXTURE PAINTING

Texture paints offer a decorative alternative to flat paint. Available in either premixed or dry, powdered latex forms, these paints can produce a wide range of stippled or stuccolike effects.

Peach-toned paint with a textured finish creates an old-world European mood in a dining room.

✦ Choose textured paints to cover seriously damaged surfaces.

✦ Practice texture painting on a piece of heavy cardboard until you get the look you want.

✦ The depth of the texture depends on the stiffness of the texture paint, the amount of paint applied to the surface, and the type of tool used to create the texture.

✦ Experiment with various applicators including brushes, trowels, whisk brooms, crumpled newspaper, and sponges.

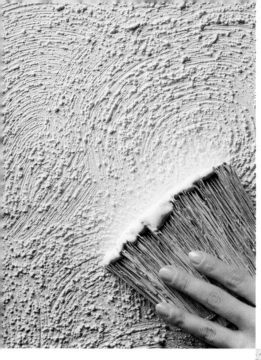

Use a whisk broom (left) to create a swirl pattern. Apply the texture paint onto the ceiling or wall with a roller, then drag the whisk broom across the surface to create the design you like.

Use sponges (right) to create a variety of textures by dabbing, dragging, or swirling. Create a two-tone stucco effect by letting one coat dry, then sponging another color on top.

Create a crow's-foot design (above) by applying texture paint with a roller, brushing it out level, and then randomly striking the surface with the flat of the brush.

Create an adobe pattern (left) by using a trowel to texture material into a series of flat and ridged surfaces.

Use a looped texture roller to create a stippled effect (right). Modify the texture by varying the pressure on your roller and the amount of paint on the surface.

painting the
EXTERIOR

A great paint job can highlight your home's best features, hide flaws, even increase its value. Before you invest considerable money and effort in painting your home, take time to plan the project carefully.

For every exterior, be it lap siding, shakes, or stucco, there are specially formulated paints and stains for the job. With the right information and the proper tools, you'll be proud of your results.

With its ceiling painted a pastel shade, this porch has a year-round summery look.

EXTERIOR SURFACES

Various surfaces call for different painting approaches. Always ask for guidance at your paint or home improvement store, where you will find many products designed specifically for certain types of exterior surface materials.

✦ Choose colors thoughtfully. There are more colors and recommended color combinations available then ever before. Depending on the style of your home, consider choosing a palette that has a main color for siding, complementary accent color for trim or architectural details, and perhaps a bold accent color for the front door.

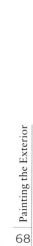

✦ Clear areas surrounding the house so you will have easy access for ladders and scaffolding. Tie back bushes and shrubs with rope, and trim branches where necessary. Cover bushes with drop cloths as you paint.

✦ The best painting weather is dry, moderately warm, and slightly breezy. Latex paint cannot be properly applied below 50°F.

✦ Damp surfaces will cause oil paint to blister and bubble.

✦ Extreme heat causes paint to crack as it dries too quickly. Always check the label and follow recommendations.

Estimating Materials

1 To estimate the amount of paint you'll need, calculate the area (height × width) of the exterior walls in square feet (or square meters). For gable, or triangular-shaped, surfaces, your formula is: width at the base of triangle × ½ height of triangle. Add them all together for your total.

2 Use these guidelines for figuring the amount of paint you will need to buy (always check label for the manufacturer's recommendations):

- ◆ raw stucco = 150 sq. ft./gal.
- ◆ painted stucco = 250 sq. ft./gal.
- ◆ unfinished wood siding = 350 sq. ft./gal.
- ◆ painted wood siding = 350 sq. ft./gal.
- ◆ new shingles = 200 sq. ft./gal.

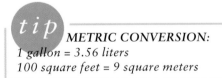

tip **METRIC CONVERSION:**
1 gallon = 3.56 liters
100 square feet = 9 square meters

Specialty Tools

In addition to brushes and rollers, there are some
tools designed specifically for exterior work.

✦ A rough surface painter looks like a flat scrub
brush with tufts of short bristles and is designed for
painting split shingles.

✦ Stucco brushes have a chiseled end and a gently
rounded mass of bristles.

✦ Shingle brushes are wide and thick at the base
with long bristles that taper to a very fine edge.

Exterior scaffolding should be created with wood
or aluminum planks. Choose 16- to 24-foot planks
to avoid frequent moves. Lay the plank across
specially designed brackets that attach to your extension ladder.

For painting exteriors with an extension ladder,
place the ladder against the house at a 75° angle.
As a rule, place the base of the ladder away from the
house at a distance that is equal to 1/4 of the ladder's
total length when extended. For instance, place the
foot of a 28-foot extension ladder approximately
7 feet from the wall. Level the ladder with wood
blocks whenever necessary.

Mildew

PROBLEM: This fungus may develop in damp areas that receive little direct sunlight.

SOLUTION: Wash the area with a chlorine bleach solution (1 part bleach: 3 parts water) or a commercial mildew remover. Rinse well and let dry.

Chalking

PROBLEM: A filmy powder of pigment may develop over time, especially when poor quality paint has been used.

SOLUTION: Wash off, using a scrub brush and power washer.

Water or Rust Stains

PROBLEM: Areas around faucets or downspouts may develop unsightly rust stains.

SOLUTION: Wash stained areas near metal surfaces with a wire brush, then sand and prime before painting. To prevent reoccurrence, clean and seal the rusty metal with a rust-inhibitor primer or clear coat.

Peeling and Chipping

PROBLEM: Loose paint may be peeling or chipping due to poor surface preparation.

SOLUTION: Scrape away loose paint, using a wire brush. Then sand and wipe clean with a damp cloth before priming.

Blistering

PROBLEM: Blistering paint is usually caused by moisture trapped behind the paint.

SOLUTION: Scrape the area, and sand smooth before priming.

Alligatoring

PROBLEM: This distinctive cracking may result when layers of old paint build up, where paint has dried too quickly, or if paint has been applied too thickly.

SOLUTION: Scrape and sand all areas before priming.

CLEANING

Every house should be cleaned thoroughly before sanding, priming, or painting. Hand-wash by working from the top down with a TSP solution and a scrub brush with a handle. Rinse with a garden hose fitted with a pistol-grip nozzle.

Wear protective gear when working with a power washer (widely available at stores supplying rental equipment). Used with your garden hose, these units project a powerful stream of water at the surface, which will loosen surface dirt as well as loose and chalking paint. Never aim a power washer in the direction of a person.

Scraping

Remove all loose paint from the surface with either a hook scraper or a chisel blade. Use a two-handed grip with a hook scraper, pulling the scraper toward you along the surface. Chisel blades are meant to be pushed under the edge of the peeling paint and away from your body. Scrape paint with horizontal motions to avoid gouging and scratching the wood. Check your home improvement store for specialized scrapers designed for use in difficult areas like carved millwork.

PREPARING SURFACES

Sanding

To smooth scraped areas or weathered surfaces, sand in the direction of the grain. For large areas, use either an orbital or belt sander. Keep three basic sandpaper grades on hand: 60-grit for coarse work, 80-grit for medium work, 100-grit for fine work. Electric drills fitted with sanding attachments may also be used, but be careful to avoid ripple marks on the surface caused by the circular motion of the sander. To work in small, hard-to-reach areas, fold a piece of sandpaper around a putty knife or block of wood; or, simply fold a piece of sandpaper and work by hand. Always remember that sanding is intended to smooth transition areas between raw wood and painted surfaces, and to remove problem spots on painted areas. Avoid oversanding unfinished wood.

tip **SAFETY:** *Use extreme caution when placing ladders near wires. Always assume every wire is a live wire, and do not touch.*

MAKING MINOR REPAIRS

There are two stages to your house-painting project: preparing the surfaces and applying the paint. Though you may be anxious to start painting, the preparation work can actually take you far more time, and requires a bit of patience and know-how. The time and effort invested in careful preparation, including patching holes, repairing cracks, scraping, and sanding, pays off in a longer-lasting, professional-quality paint finish.

◀ *Caulking*

Use a paintable siliconized acrylic caulk to seal seams, open joints, and gaps around door and window trim. Wait the recommended amount of time before priming.

> *tip* **TECHNICAL:** *Apply primers only when you know you can finish your paint job soon after. Some primers begin to deteriorate quickly when left exposed. As a rule, the faster the drying time, the faster the deterioration. Check the label for recommended drying times, then proceed with painting.*

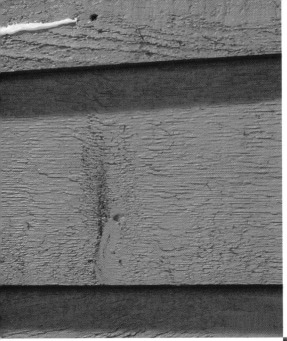

Repairing Splits and Cracks

Repair splits and cracks in wood siding with epoxy wood glue. Apply the glue to both sides of the split; then press the board back together. Clean off any excess glue. Reinforce the repair by driving galvanized deck screws into the wood on each side of the split.

Repairing Holes in Wood

Fill small nail holes and shallow gouges in wood with epoxy wood filler. Let dry, and sand smooth. For metal and vinyl siding, use tinted exterior caulk in a color to match.

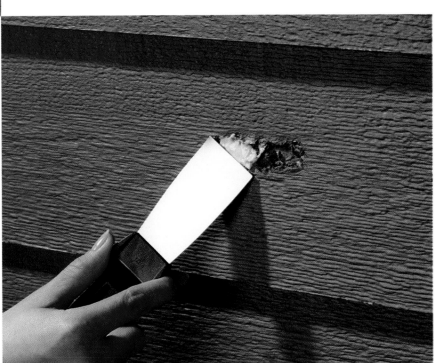

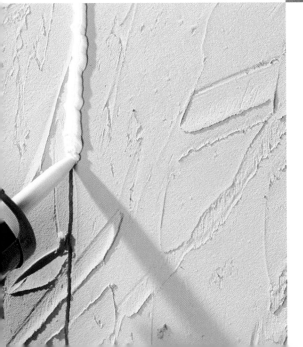

Repairing Stucco and Masonry

Patch cracks in stucco, using concrete caulk. Overfill the crack, and then feather it flush with the surrounding area. Allow the caulk to set completely before painting. Ready-mixed products, available in home improvement and hardware stores, are used for patching small holes in stucco, masonry, and concrete.

APPLYING THE PAINT – FOLLOW A PLAN

✦ Begin by painting your siding, or walls, first, then paint windows, doors, and trim.

✦ Paint from the top down. Apply flat paint before using any gloss paints (it's easier to clean up mistakes made with flat paint).

✦ Don't stop painting in the middle of a wall; always choose a natural break, such as a corner or the edge of an architectural feature, if you need to stop.

✦ Plan your work day so you are not painting in direct sunlight at any time, and so your paint has time to dry before overnight dew becomes a problem.

1 For lap siding, paint the bottom edges of the boards with a 4" (10 cm) paintbrush held flat against the wall. Complete this step for several rows of siding within your reach. Then paint the broad faces of those boards, using the same brush. Paint in long strokes, unloading all the paint from the brush with each stroke. Reload the brush and paint from the other direction with the next stroke, feathering into the end of the previous stroke. Work from the top of the wall down.

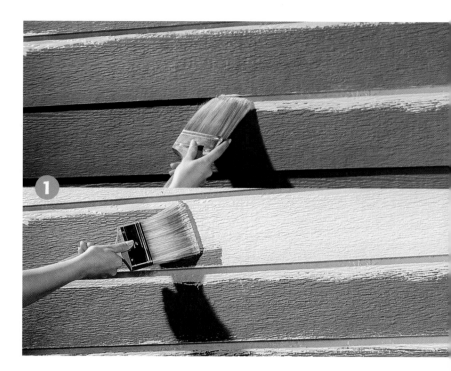

2 To paint trim, first decide whether you will use a "face-off" or "wrap" technique. Facing off (below, left) is when you paint the outer edges of the trim the same color as the siding, then paint the face and inside edges with the trim color. Wrapping (below, right), which is slightly more difficult, means painting all areas of the trim, including the edge along the siding, with the trim color.

3 Open sash windows before painting, sliding the upper half down and the lower half up about halfway. Paint the upper rail of the bottom sash first, then paint the stiles, muntins, and crossbars. Slide the window down slightly, and finish painting the bottom half. Next paint the top half of the window, moving top to bottom.

4 To paint doors, prop open at a slight angle and begin with the hinge edge. Wipe the face of the door clean of paint as you go. Next, paint the face of the door, working top to bottom. Work quickly to maintain a wet edge, since any lap marks (or other mistakes) will be very visible. The lock edge of the door should be painted the same color as the interior area into which the door opens.

face off ←

wrap ←

Painting Other Siding Types

For vertical-panel siding, such as board-and-batten (top, left), first paint the edges and then the faces of the narrow top boards (battens), using a narrow paintbrush. Then paint the large, broad panels between the battens, using a roller or 4" (10 cm) brush. If the panel surface is rough in texture, use a roller cover with a ⅝" (1.5 cm) nap.

Shake or shingle siding (top, right), because of its uneven texture, is difficult to paint with a brush. Spray painting is recommended for very rough, irregularly spaced shakes. For shakes with relatively smooth surfaces, paint the bottom edges of several rows with a brush. Then paint the flat grooved surfaces in vertical strokes, using a large exterior painting pad. The deep nap of the pad reaches into the grooved surface of the shakes for even application of paint.

PAINTING MASONRY AND CONCRETE

General Tips

◆ Wash surfaces first to remove dirt, grease, and mildew (see page 74).

◆ Remove any old paint with a stiff-bristle brush. If there is *efflorescence,* or a chalky residue, on the surface, scrub the surface with the brush and a solution of 10% muriatic acid.

◆ Use a waterproofing compound, available at paint and home improvement stores, for basement walls where dampness may be a problem; apply the finish coat (bottom, right) over the waterproofing.

◆ Choose a primer specifically formulated to seal masonry or concrete. Paint relatively smooth stucco siding (bottom, left), using a paint roller with a ⅝" (1.5 cm) nap. Touch up with a paintbrush, if necessary. Spray painting is recommended for rough stucco siding.

◆ Apply paint to a cleaned and primed surface in a crisscross pattern, using a long-nap roller. Distribute paint evenly by rolling across, then up and down, the crisscross pattern. Paint one workable section at a time before moving on to the next.

all about
STAINS

Stains enhance the natural beauty of wood with rich color. Whether you are staining a wood floor, interior woodwork, or your home's exterior, there are stains, sealers, and combination products to help you do the job right. Learn about the products available to you, and determine the look you want for your home.

Floors with a honey-hued stain capture sunlight in a hall.

STAINS AND VARNISHES

There are many stains and varnishes on the market, including both water-base and oil-base varieties. These products are most often used to color, seal, and protect wood surfaces like trim, floors, and furniture.

Stains

Stains allow you to apply color to wood surfaces without covering the natural beauty of the wood grain. Stains actually soak into wood and must be finished with a protective top coat, or varnish. Today, staining products are available in not just traditional wood tones, but a wide variety of colors.

Varnishes

All varnishes, including the most commonly known, polyurethane, are formulated to provide a durable, clear coat over unfinished or stained wood, or over painted surfaces. These finishing products are available in various sheens, from satin to high-gloss. Typically, you will need to apply at least two coats of varnish to achieve an optimum finish. Clear acrylic finishing products are not recommended for use on floors.

Dark-stained floors give a stylish finish to a dining room (left); an armoire with a striking painted, stained, and stenciled decoration is an eye-catching work of art (below).

Stain and Polyurethane Combinations

These one-step products are designed to provide both color and clear-coat finish for wood surfaces like trim and furniture. Most can be cleaned up with soap and water.

Drying Times

As a rule of thumb, water-base stains and varnishes will dry more quickly than oil-base products. Some water-base stains and varnishes dry in 1 hour or less, while oil-base stains can take up to 6 hours; some cannot be recoated for 24 hours. Always check the can's label, which should clearly state the product's drying time and the recommended time to wait before reapplying the product.

tip **TECHNICAL:** *Always test the final effect of your stain or varnish on a piece of similar scrap wood or on a hidden area of the surface you want to finish.*

Staining Interior Surfaces

1 Clean the woodwork with a TSP solution to remove wax, grease, and dirt. Rinse, and allow to dry.

2 Remove existing paint or varnish with a commercial stripper, or sand with a medium paper; finish with a fine-grit paper, and wipe clean with a tack cloth.

3 Working in the direction of the grain, apply stain with a clean, lint-free cloth or a synthetic-bristle brush. Use a natural brush when applying oil-base stains.

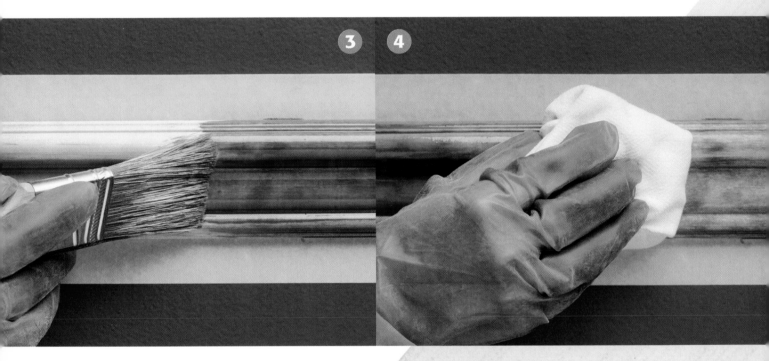

4 Wipe off excess stain with a clean cloth. The final appearance of the wood depends on how long you allow the stain to penetrate the wood. For a very rich, deep color, reapply stain after 12 hours, and allow to dry.

5 If staining has raised the grain of the wood, sand lightly with a fine-grit paper, and wipe clean with a tack cloth.

6 Apply a clear acrylic or polyurethane finish to seal and protect the wood surface.

tip **TECHNIQUE:** *While using a lint-free cloth to apply stain is sometimes easier, you will use more stain than you would if you were applying stain with a brush. Wear gloves to protect your hands when applying any staining product with a cloth.*

APPLYING EXTERIOR STAINS

General Considerations

◆ As a rule, rough surfaces hold more color than smooth surfaces.

◆ Weathered wood will absorb more color than new wood.

◆ Heavily pigmented, or colored, stains will mask problem areas better than more transparent stains.

◆ Because pigment in stain helps block the sun's damaging ultraviolet rays, choose more opaque products for areas exposed to constant sun.

◆ Clear wood preservatives applied to unfinished wood will help prevent graying and fading.

◆ Clear coatings, like varnish and polyurethane, will preserve the color of natural wood and also protect the surface.

◆ Stain (or paint) wood trim and windows before staining wall surfaces.

◆ On large wall areas, work from top to bottom, applying stain in the direction of the grain. For horizontal boards, stain the bottom of the boards first, then the face. Stain the entire length of the board whenever possible, and always maintain a wet edge.

Staining Exterior Surfaces

1 Smooth out any rough areas, using an orbital sander, before applying stain to decking boards, railings, or stair treads. Vacuum the wood to remove the sawdust before applying the stain.

tip **TECHNICAL:** *Use deep-penetrating solid-color stains for siding, fences, shakes, trim, and pressure-treated wood. For decks, choose semi-transparent stain or deck and siding protector. Read can labels carefully to be sure you are buying the right product.*

2 Test the surface before you stain by pouring a few drops of water onto the wood. If the water beads up on the surface, the wood will not absorb the stain. If the water is absorbed into the wood, go ahead and apply a small amount of stain as a test patch in a hidden area; allow to dry before checking the final color.

3 When staining decks, stain rails and posts first. For deck boards, work the full length of two or three boards at a time to avoid lap marks. Work the stain evenly toward the stairs or door, and do not let stain sit in puddles on the surface.

cleaning up RIGHT

At the end of a paint job, you may choose to throw away roller covers or inexpensive foam brushes, but many items should be cleaned and stored for future use.

It is extremely important to dispose of all oil-base paint products in an environmentally safe manner. Check with your local municipality to find out where the hazardous waste sites are located and designate one morning to bring all your hazardous painting waste to this site. Never toss oil-base paint cans or solvents into your household trash.

CLEAN THE ROOM

✦ Remove painter's tape from window glass, and scrape any dried paint drips off the glass.

✦ Replace all hardware, switch plates, and light fixtures.

✦ Roll up drop cloths and plastic drapes, and store them in a dry spot.

✦ Remove dried-on paint spatters on carpet by snipping out with sharp scissors (do not attempt to wipe up paint when it's still wet).

✦ Sand out any paint drips on unfinished wood.

Cleaning Your Tools

1 Clean brushes used for water-base paints by soaking them in soapy water. Use a brush-cleaning comb to thoroughly clean and realign the bristles.

2 Dry your brushes by waving or spinning them vigorously. Wrap the clean and dry brushes in brown paper and hang them on a hook or nail to store.

3 Scrape paint from roller covers with a roller-cleaning tool, widely available in paint and home improvement stores.

4 Soak the cover in a soapy water solution to remove water-base paints. Rinse the cover with clean water and squeeze dry by hand. Or spin the cover dry, using a spinning tool, available at paint and home improvement stores.

5 Stand roller covers on end overnight to dry completely, taking care not to let the cover touch anything. Store roller covers on end wrapped in plastic or brown paper.

6 Rinse buckets and pans with soapy water, then scrub away remaining paint with a cleaning pad. Dry and store.

STORING PAINT PRODUCTS

✦ It is always wise to keep at least a small amount of every paint color and finishing product that you have used, for touch-ups later on. Transfer small amounts of paint that would otherwise dry out in a gallon can into a small, clean glass jar with a tight-fitting lid. Label clearly, and store according to manufacturer's recommendations. If you have more than one opened can, combine all leftover paint in one can and reseal tightly by pounding the lid into place with a hammer. Use a thick cloth to protect the lid from the hammer.

✦ If you have used thinners in your paint project, recycle them for use in another project. Leave the thinner to stand for a week so it will clear, with paint residue settling to the bottom. Pour the thinner into a bottle or glass jar, and label clearly. Dispose of the paint residue by adding kitty litter or other absorbent product to the jar; cover the jar and bring to the hazardous waste disposal site.

Disposing of Paint

When in doubt, treat paint products as hazardous waste and dispose of them accordingly. Never pour any paint products like oil-base paint, solvents, or thinners down the drain or outside on the ground. Rags soaked in solvents should be set outside to dry, never left inside, as they are potentially combustible. Bag the rags after they have completely dried, and bring them to your hazardous waste disposal site.

Soak up small amounts of water-base paint with kitty litter, then place in your household trash. Paint cans should be rinsed thoroughly and then recycled.

INTERIOR PAINTS

Flat Interior Latex
Flat sheen
One-coat coverage
Superior washability
Hides minor
imperfections

Ceiling White Interior Latex
Once-coat coverage
Flat sheen
Spatter resistant

**Satin Wall & Trim
Interior Latex**
Satin sheen
One-coat coverage
Superior washability
Fade Resistant

Winter Whites Interior Latex
Available in flat, satin, semi-
gloss, and high-gloss sheens
High hiding
Washable

**Kitchen & Bath Interior
Latex**
Semi-gloss sheen
One-coat coverage
Super scrub formula
Stain & mildew resistant

Satin Enamel Latex
For exterior or interior use
Elegant satin sheen
Superior durability
Soap & water cleanup

Playhouse Interior Latex
Low -gloss enamel
Easy cleaning
Super scrub formula
One-coat coverage

Gloss Enamel Latex
For exterior or interior use
Brilliant gloss sheen
Superior durability
Soap & water cleanup

EXTERIOR PAINTS

Satin Acrylic Latex
Low-gloss satin sheen
One-coat coverage
Weather & mildew resistant
Blister, fade, & chalk resistant
Ideal for aluminum siding

Flat Acrylic Latex
Flat sheen
One-coat coverage
Weather & mildew resistant
Blister, fade, & chalk resistant

Gloss Acrylic Latex
Medium gloss sheen
One-coat coverage
Weather and mildew resistant
Blister, fade, & chalk resistant

Interior Latex Drywall Primer
- Seals drywall for uniform topcoat
- Quick drying, low odor
- Soap & water cleanup

Exterior Latex House Paint Primer
- Weather and mildew resistant
- For masonry, aluminum, and vinyl

ZAP
- Mildew resistant
- Fast drying
- Interior/exterior sealer

Deep Color Primer
- For interior or exterior use
- Tints to match topcoat
- Soap & water cleanup

Interior Polyurethane
- Mar resistant, durable protection
- Semi-gloss finish
- Ideal for floors
- Clean up with mineral spirits

STAINS & SEALERS

Interior Stain & Poly
- Gloss finish
- One-step wood finish
- Fast drying
- Soap & water cleanup

Waterproofing Semi-transparent Stain
- Exterior oil formula
- Water repellent; fade resistant
- Mildew resistant

Interior Wood Stain
- Penetrates, stains, seals
- For bare, unfinished or unsealed interior wood
- Clean up with mineral spirits

Exterior Oil/Acrylic Solid Color Stain
- Deep penetrating formula
- Water repellent; fade & mildew resistant

Interior Clear Acrylic
- Long-lasting durability
- Fast drying
- Soap & water cleanup
- Non-yellowing
- Not for use on floors

Deck & Siding Protector
- Deep penetrating oil formula
- Screens out U.V. rays
- Mildew resistant

Index